# The Nationalist

Iris Schindler

ISBN: 979-8-89525-929-0

# Dedication

This is to my father, Juan Elias Bonilla (January 10$^{th}$, 1924), the person who stayed in my life like a rock, someone I am forever proud to have as part of my life.

And to my beloved sister, Mickie (1949-20), who was killed by a drunk driver. I have loved and cherish every moment with you.

# Acknowledgment

I would like to express my deepest gratitude to my family, whose love and support have been my greatest source of inspiration. To my parents, whose unwavering dedication to our education and well-being taught me the value of hard work and perseverance.

A special thanks to my friends and colleagues who provided invaluable feedback and encouragement throughout the writing process. Your insights and support have been instrumental in bringing this book to life.

Lastly, to my readers, thank you for embarking on this journey with me. Your support and enthusiasm make all the effort worthwhile.

# Contents

# About the Author

Born in Puerto Rico as the youngest of three girls, Iris Schindler stood out in her family from the very beginning. While her parents and sisters all had black hair, she was born with strikingly blond hair, a trait that baffled her mother. This unique trait contributed to her special bond with her mother.

Iris shared a close relationship with her sister Mickie and shared her tomboy spirit, and the two were inseparable. They spent their days playing baseball with the neighborhood boys and were so inseparable that every photo of them together shows them holding hands. In contrast, their oldest sister preferred the indoors.

Iris and her sisters attended Catholic institutions throughout their education, starting with daycare and continuing through kindergarten, grade school, and finally, high school. Their mother worked diligently in a factory to ensure they received a proper education, instilling in them the values of hard work and the importance of learning.

This dedication to education and family is a cornerstone of Iris' life and work, reflecting the values and experiences that have shaped her storytelling.

# Preface

"The Nationalist" is a tribute to a man whose life was defined by strength and determination. Born in Puerto Rico, Iris' father, Juan Elias, faced numerous challenges from an early age, including the hardships of the Great Depression and the loss of a loved one. To support his family, he showed remarkable resourcefulness.

As he grew older, he mastered the craft of carpentry, building a successful career, and starting a family despite economic difficulties. His dedication extended beyond his personal life to political activism, fighting for Puerto Rican independence even when it was dangerous.

Through it all, he remained a devoted family man and community leader, and his influence and courage continued to inspire those around him.

This book celebrates his journey, showing how perseverance and resilience can impact many lives.

# Chapter 1:

# Early Years in Puerto Rico

I was born into a family with a rich history in the beautiful country of Puerto Rico. My grandfather, born and bred in San Juan, was a merchant who quickly established himself as one of the top sellers of a wide range of men's goods, from suits and shoes to socks. His success as a merchant stemmed from his unflinching resolve, resourcefulness, and sharp business acumen. He had bought his own store, an establishment that solely catered to high-end clientele, and the quality of the products he sold was renowned throughout. His reputation for offering high-quality suits and exceptional customer service elevated his store to a prominent position in our community in San Juan.

My grandfather had eight children, with my father being the third in the family. The formative years of my father, Juan Elias, who stood out from the rest of his siblings, were marked by intriguing developments and challenges that would significantly shape his character and life trajectory, and it all started when he was an infant. As a young child, he faced a notable delay in communication, unlike most children his age. Until he turned three, he remained nonverbal, which became a cause of concern for his family. By age four, he still hadn't found his voice completely, mumbling words and faltering every time he spoke.

However, at age five, something remarkable happened—he began to talk. This transformation marked the beginning of a trait that would be his defining feature for the rest of his life—a constant, intelligent ability to carry a conversation. His father's influence would soon complement this emerging articulateness in his speech.

His influence on my father's upbringing was profound. His achievements and character left an indelible mark on his formative years, shaping not only his understanding of business but also the principles, values, and work ethic he religiously follows today.

"You see these suits, son?" my grandfather once said to him, "Each one represents quality and hard work. Always strive for excellence."

"Why do you work so much, Papa?" asked my father innocently.

Taking a deep breath, he said, "Because I want to provide for our family, and I want you to understand the value of hard work and how a man should always put his family first, even before himself."

My grandfather believed in leading by example and instilled in my father and his siblings the values of diligence and persistence. From a tender age, my father witnessed his commitment to the business. He worked long hours and demonstrated a strong work ethic, which became a guiding principle for him. My grandfather's dedication was not just about financial success; it was a matter of pride, a commitment to excellence, and a sense of responsibility to our family and community.

The most profound influence my grandfather had on my father's upbringing was his character. He was known for his integrity, honesty, and fairness in business dealings. He treated customers, employees, and suppliers with respect and kindness. His reputation for ethical conduct preceded him, and it was something he cherished deeply. This moral compass left a lasting impression on my father when he learned that success should never come at the expense of one's values and principles.

My father had seen all of this from a young age, as he had grown up in this environment, being exposed to the inner workings of the business from a young age. My grandfather's success, his steadfast work ethic, financial prowess, commitment to the community, and emphasis on education all left an enduring effect on my father, who later imparted these values to us growing up.

My grandfather proved to be a successful businessman in the world of men's suits. But he wasn't alone in this endeavor; he was in business with his two brothers, solidifying a legacy of success in the world of fine clothing. With a thriving business, they ensured that there was no expense spared. He had enjoyed a life of luxury, attending fancy parties, political events, and social gatherings. But it was about more than just business for him. He made sure that his daughters had the means to indulge in social events like visiting a W 10 bar. Their mother, thanks to his efforts, had the financial resources to create stunning dresses for these special occasions.

However, their fortunes took a drastic turn when the Great Depression swept across the country. My grandfather, who had been instrumental in their prosperity, tragically lost all of their wealth. The despair and financial ruin ultimately led to a heart-wrenching event—when my grandfather committed suicide.

My grandfather's emphasis on education was unwavering. He believed in the value of knowledge and education. However, when my grandfather passed away and the family business went under, my father had to make a difficult decision. He quit school to help support the family, underlining the sacrifices he made for our family's well-being. My grandfather's business acumen was another invaluable lesson that my father religiously practiced after his death. He was taught the importance of adaptability in business and how to pivot when necessary. When my father made the tough decision to quit school, he constructed a cart for selling goods, a small step in a life that would take him in unexpected directions.

When my father was a child, he had a fiery temper, a trait he would carry with him throughout his life, but it was not directed toward his father. Instead, he exhibited a deep sense of reverence and admiration for him. His father's words and guidance carried immense weight, shaping his actions and decisions. When his father offered advice or warnings, he would heed them with the utmost obedience. If his father said, "Don't do that," there was no question or debate about whether to do it or not; there was only one road to take. My grandfather's influence was a cornerstone for all his endeavors, and his memory continues to inspire him to this day.

There was a profound reverence for all the wisdom he acquired from his father. Their relationship wasn't just one of father and son; it was a connection built on mutual respect and a shared sense of responsibility. This deep respect for his father's wisdom and guidance laid the foundation for my father's own values and convictions. The untimely death of his father was a pivotal moment in his life, one that ignited a burning determination within him to work tirelessly for his family. His father's passing left a permanent scar on his heart and mind, driving him to honor his father's memory by embodying the values and principles his father had imparted.

His father's words, spoken with wisdom, echoed in his ears even after his father was no longer physically present. He recalled the times when his father had emphasized the importance of hard work, responsibility, and dedication. Those words had never been mere admonitions but were, in fact, a blueprint for life, a legacy handed down from one generation to the next. His father's commitment to their family's well-being, diligence with work, and sense of duty had been the bedrock upon which their family stood. These values were the very essence of my grandfather's character, and they now became the guiding stars for my father.

The pain of losing his father, coupled with the financial hardships that befell the family in the wake of the Great Depression, instilled in him the urgency to uplift his family out of ruin. He felt an immense responsibility to carry the torch that his father had carried before him. This sense of duty, rooted in his father's teachings, drove him to work hard, persevere through adversity, and ensure that his family's needs were met.

When he was seventeen, he and his brothers went for a swim, and the unimaginable happened. A massive tidal hit them, and in a desperate attempt to save his brother, my father was wrenched away by the rough waters. The search for his brother's body became a harrowing ordeal; it was a relentless pursuit, deploying helicopters, divers, and every resource available, which would turn out to be futile. My father's uncle played a key role during this wearisome time, providing the financial means to support the search. A resourceful group of farmers finally located his brother's body. This traumatic event and the guilt it left behind became a heavy burden for my father to carry in his life journey.

Throughout the tumultuous years, their financial condition worsened. The loss of his brother and their financial constraints all contributed to the family's desolation. However, his uncle, who offered vital support during these challenging times, played a significant role in his upbringing since then. His uncle was a source of guidance and aid, especially now that his family was on his own.

My father saw the suffering and hardships that ordinary people faced during the period of the Great Depression, and it intensified his desire to create a better future, not just for his family but for all the people of Puerto Rico. It was soon after that he believed he had found his true calling: to become involved in a cause greater than himself. At the age of seventeen, he decided to join the Nationalist Party, which was advocating for Puerto Rican independence and social justice, resonating deeply within him. The party's commitment to Puerto Rican sovereignty and the fight for a more equitable society aligned with his own values and aspirations for liberation.

His choice to join the Nationalist Party was a significant turning point in his life, as it marked the beginning of his journey into the world of political activism. In the face of challenges and financial struggles, my father was able to find the strength to persevere, carrying forward his father's memory and teachings. He channeled his grief into commitment, ensuring that his family would not just survive but thrive. His father's words became a beacon of guidance and a powerful catalyst for his hard work and resilience, a remnant of the everlasting influence of a father's love and wisdom even after his passing.

# Chapter 2:

# The Great Depression and Family Tragedy

The Great Depression of the 1930s was a dark period filled with economic hardship that affected families across the United States and beyond. For my family, it was no different. My father's family was among the hundreds of thousands of families who were plunged into living on the poverty line. It cast a long and enduring shadow on their lives, one that would follow them for years.

In the midst of the Great Depression, our family's business, which had once thrived, found itself grappling with the crippling economic challenges of the time. The Depression had brought about widespread unemployment, economic downturns, and financial instability. Customers who had once frequented my grandfather's establishment and were his dear and old friends now stopped visiting the shop entirely. Our store was the only one of its kind in the area at that time, and that's what they relied on to stay afloat. Given the loyalty of their customers and the quality of the clothes, my grandfather retained hope that he could tread the rocky waters of economic despair. But, as fate would have it, no one was spared from the widespread financial downturn.

Huge brands and franchises were closing left, right, and center. I suppose my grandfather was naïve to think that he and his store could make it through unscathed, but truth be told, even if he had known this was going to happen, he still couldn't have prevented it; such was the devastating impact of the Great Depression.

Soon, he saw a dramatic decline in business. This sudden and severe downturn was a severe blow to our family's once-thriving business, along with countless others, which struggled to survive. Tragically, the weight of these financial burdens took a severe toll on my grandfather. Unable to bear the anguish and despair of their financial downfall, he made the heart-wrenching decision to end his own life. His suicide was a devastating event that sent shockwaves throughout the family, leaving them not only emotionally shattered but also coming to terms with the practical implications of their loss.

The impact of his passing on the family was profound, to say the least. The sudden loss of a father and husband in such tragic circumstances left them with an enduring sense of grief, guilt, and confusion. My father was one of eight siblings who were left to the mercy of the ruthless world, now at their own devices to navigate it themselves. While my great-uncle was there to cushion the blow by being the father figure that they lost, all of them still craved the presence of their own father.

Aside from the emotional spiral my father and his siblings were sent into, the financial ramifications were equally significant. With the family business going under due to the Depression, the loss of the primary breadwinner intensified their financial distress tenfold. The economic hardships of the era, coupled with the loss of my grandfather's income, meant that the family was shoved into dire financial circumstances. They were forced to confront the harsh realities of making ends meet during one of the most challenging periods in history. The Great Depression was a never-ending storm that stripped away any semblance of stability in the family.

Thankfully, they had my great uncle, who played a crucial role during one of the hardest periods of their lives; he was there for us through thick and thin, assuring them that he would be by their side no matter what. He was a remarkable man who owned a unique business – a combination of a jewelry store and a pawn shop. This business became more than just a source of income; it became a symbol of hope and support for our family and the community during those trying times. People were faced with the heartbreaking decision to part with their most precious possessions just to make ends meet. It was a time when wedding bands and cherished heirlooms were hidden away, left to gather dust and memories, and it was also a time when many found themselves in dire need of immediate financial assistance.

People in the community would come to him with their most treasured items, hoping to exchange them for financial relief. Lucky for them, he was a man of empathy and compassion. When they came to him, desperately in need of money to feed their families or keep a roof over their heads, he always responded with kindness. He understood the gravity of the times and the sacrifices people were making to survive. He didn't exploit their vulnerability, nor did he take advantage of their unfortunate circumstances. Instead, he offered a helping hand, giving them a fair deal that allowed them to provide for their families. His business became a beacon of hope, a place where people could find not only financial relief but also a sense of dignity in a world that had been turned upside down. His generosity extended to my father's family the most, and they were forever grateful for the security and support he provided.

Before my grandfather passed, my father's sisters had been accustomed to a certain lifestyle; it was disappointing to my father and great-uncle that they couldn't provide them with the luxuries that they had gotten used to. My father, who was still a teenager at the time, found himself thrust into adulthood early on, with the weight of family responsibilities now falling on his young shoulders. My great-uncle ensured that our sisters had all that they needed and that they wouldn't miss out on anything their hearts desired. The responsibility of putting food on the table and ensuring our family's survival largely fell on the shoulders of the other boys, too, while our sisters enjoyed a more comfortable life.

My father was in high school at the time, an age when most were still focused on their education and other trivial matters like dating and mingling with friends. However, the sudden loss of my grandfather brought about a stark reality that demanded his immediate attention. The weight of this responsibility was immense, but my father faced it, knowing he had no other option, and his sense of duty took over. Ensuring that there was a warm meal on the table three times a day, a roof over their heads, and clothes on their backs was the least he could do for his family.

Something changed in him the day my grandfather died; he became a responsible grownup overnight. He decided to start working, lending a helping hand to my uncle, and the rest of the boys in the family followed suit.

He understood the gravity of the situation and remembered the lessons of hard work and commitment instilled in him by his own father. The words of his father were embedded deep in his memory – to be a man, to work hard, and to ensure the well-being of the family. In the face of financial hardships and the weight of responsibility, my father's untiring commitment to his family and the principles instilled by his own father guided him.

With a fierce resolve, my father took up a series of rather humble jobs to make ends meet. The weight of this responsibility didn't daunt him; it motivated him to take action. If my father managed to make twenty-five cents, it meant a meal for his family of eight, nine with my mother included. He had a strong work ethic, and he was relentless in his pursuit of providing for them. His determination was unflinching in the face of destitution and adversity, embodying the lessons imparted to him by his father.

One of the clever ways he sought to provide for our family was by setting up a makeshift business. Given his craftiness and resourcefulness, he made a cart to push, and with a block of ice and fruits harvested from our backyard, he began making ice cones. This small, homemade enterprise became a source of income for him and his big family. He would create his own syrup using the fruits from our trees, and then he would take his cart to town to sell these ice cones for just two pennies each. This modest venture became a lifeline for our family during those challenging times. Every penny he earned was precious, and it all went toward putting food on our table.

Still only a teenager, my father didn't limit himself to selling ice cones; he expanded his skill set further. He ventured into construction work and dipped his toes in carpentry, learning valuable trades that allowed him to earn a living. Soon, he became a skilled carpenter, involved in the construction of houses, buildings, and various projects. These skills provided him with another source of income and broadened his horizons. His journey was one filled with sacrifice, hard work, and dedication to providing for his family, even in the most trying of circumstances. His ability to turn adversity into opportunity and his resourcefulness became a legacy that inspires me to this day.

# Chapter 3:

# A Young Entrepreneur

The best possible way to describe my father is through the phrase "jack of all trades." He was skilled in anything that one could think of. Not only that, but he would do it better. You could ask him to bake a cake from scratch, and he would do it perfectly on his first try. He made everything look so much better and was an incredibly intelligent man. He wasn't privileged enough to get proper schooling, but he used to read encyclopedias. I would like to think he was gifted.

As a child, he always had a concept of helping around the family. He would be one step ahead with his ideas, and as the creative genius he was, he would make money out of them. Because of his limitless abilities, he had created an amazing syrup recipe for the ice cream cones that he had decided to sell just to feed his family properly every evening. He wanted a good dinner and made sure all his siblings were fed at night. He would make twenty-five cents, and on the days he wasn't able to, his distress would be visible. He was once able to give life to a cart that he had built, and after that, he decided to work at a place where people were building houses and got into that. It is remarkable how he would just observe the people working there and then copy what they did. That is how he was able to perfectly master his skill.

I am not aware of the economic conditions that he was brought up in, but he felt strongly about his brother, who had lost his life.

His brother had drowned while they were out swimming, and it made him believe that he was responsible for his death. When his brother had drowned, my father's uncle sought out divers to look for him. He also got in contact with the search and rescue teams, who sent out helicopters to look for the body. He also refused to let his sister, who is my father's mother, bury her son.

The body, bloated about seven times its size, was eventually discovered by some farmers who were able to do so through their own means. They had a hard time getting him into the boat because of the weight, but they did. They brought my uncle home to my grandmother's house to have him buried in their plot. My father was terribly traumatized because of this incident, and he could never even say his name without crying his eyes out. I wonder if this is the reason why he felt that he had to take care of his family by any means possible.

Back in Puerto Rico, my father built two houses, one for my mother and one for his older sister, Hope, and her husband. It was just next door to his, and they looked like dollhouses. People drove up from everywhere in Puerto Rico just to see the beautiful houses. He made them with extra effort, and selling those houses made great money when we had to move to Chicago in 1953. They were sold for $1200. This money was the key to our new beginning. He also left behind the Nationalist Party because he wanted to start fresh with my mother and the three of us. At that time, I was only three years old.

When he came to America, my father got a job right away at a carpentry place. He was employed where people would build cabinets for kitchens. He would give his work a touch of his personality, and people were madly in love with every piece he created. He was like an artist that people greatly admired.

I remember him telling us one of the stories from his workplace. It was always something we would anticipate as it was entertaining to listen to. A friend of his taught him how to order a ham and cheese sandwich for lunch. He ordered it so many times that there was a time when he started getting sick of it. Then his friend asked him if he had ever tried a hotdog, to which my father, with a doubtful look, told him that he had not eaten dog meat before. When his friend got the hotdog, my father opened the wrapped food and looked at it for a few seconds. As if he had the wits of an experienced improv comedian, he asked him which part of the dog he had gotten. Now, I don't know if this is a real story or if he just made it up to make us laugh, but either way, he succeeded in doing so.

After moving so many times, my parents finally decided to settle in the north side of Chicago. They had to sell their house for a thousand dollars to be able to pay for the month. My mother prioritized education above everything else, so she admitted us to a Catholic school. Out of all our cousins, we were the only ones who used to attend a Catholic school, and my mother worked really hard to provide us with a good education.

My parents were able to get jobs despite their poor English language skills. My dad worked as a carpenter, and my mother was hired at the Ajax factory and received quarterly bonuses, which sometimes would be more than her salary. We weren't poor, but we didn't have a lot of money either. A year later, my mother was employed at Dr. Schholl's, where she made $1.10 an hour. That was a lot of money back in the 1950s, and she worked there for 17 years. Since she was so busy working and we were quite young, we always had a babysitter to look after us when she was away.

My oldest sibling started school two months after arriving in Chicago. He didn't speak much English, but as young kids, we learned fast. Being the youngest, I was just learning how to talk, so I was easily able to learn both languages at the same time. I remember when Mickie, my sister, and I were outside, we would speak English, but the second we walked into the house, we were speaking Spanish without giving it a second thought.

The value of money faded away in the excitement that Christmas brought to our house during our first year living in Chicago. The festive season, a time when magic seemed to dance in the air, brought a flood of memories that money couldn't buy. Wrapped in the nostalgia of childhood, each Christmas held the promise of wonder.

Under the twinkling lights of our little Christmas tree, a mystery awaited us. As we ran towards it, we found presents. Ecstatic, we started tearing down the wrapping paper one by one. The presents had won our hearts. There were dolls with porcelain faces, delicate tea sets, doll buggies, cutouts, coloring books, dresses that I couldn't take my eyes off, and comfortable new underwear, socks, and shoes. The bounty was a testament to the generosity of a make-believe Santa Claus who sprinkled our lives with joy.

Late at night, my parents would carefully wrap each of the gifts with love, hiding them away in the trunk of our family car while we slept in the comfort of our beds. When it was time to play Santa Claus, my father would go take the grocery cart that was used back then to bring groceries home, and he would make a few runs to make sure that he made prints on the snow with the cart. He would pretend to be enthralled as he told us about the tracks that Santa had left when he visited us to deliver the presents.

To think that my parents were so prepared and meticulously planned this surprise just to see the smiles and glee on our faces. In those moments, the true wealth of Christmas unfolded—not in the price tags but in the love, creativity, and caprice that adorned each carefully orchestrated detail.

My father was a great man. Unlike the typical Puerto Rican man, who let the women do the chores of the house, he would take care of my mother. After hours of work, he would come home and take part in the housework. Whenever he saw my mother working hard in the kitchen, he would join her and lend a helping hand. At times, he would give us girls our baths while my mother cooked, cleaned, and got our clothes ready for the next day of school.

He was vocal about his empathy and love toward my mother and never hesitated to show it. The same went with his temper; he would easily get fired up over the smallest things. My uncles and aunts knew about it all too well, and they made sure not to tease or make fun of him. This temper of his somewhat distanced me from him. It was frightening to me, but as I grew old and had kids of my own, I came to realize what it was about. I am glad that I later formed a close bond with him and cherished the time we spent together.

# Chapter 4:

# Meeting My Mother

The story about how my parents got together seems like a slice-of-life romance straight out of a comfort show. I would like to say that my father is a passionate romantic. He was the kind of man all women would swoon over. Back in Puerto Rico, my mother and father were both working. While my mother worked at a bridal shop, my father would walk by it every evening after he got off work.

It was perhaps love at first sight for my father, who would wave at my mother whenever he walked past the shop. She noticed and found it weird, so she ignored it. However, this didn't faze him, and he waved at her every day until she finally gave in and slightly raised her hand to give a little wave back. It must have felt like an accomplishment to my father, and it got him fired up.

His excitement grew as he wished to lock eyes with her once again. Later, though, he was met with a different situation. This time, when he saw her, she was walking with a guy. The sight alerted him and left him feeling a tug in his heart. Yet, he walked towards them impulsively with his chest puffed out like a hawk.

"You've got a pretty girl," he said, looking at him dead in the eyes.

"You bet I do," the guy replied.

"Well, I'm gonna steal her away from you," my father announced with a smirk.

"Oh, you can try," the guy responded.

The seemingly casual banter had suddenly turned into a chess game in which you get to keep the queen if you win. My father, driven by passion, was able to figure out where my mother lived and went over to her house. Her father was there, and right after they came to know of each other's presence, my father went straight to the point. Without a single thought, he asked if it was okay to date his daughter.

When my mother came back from work later that evening, she saw the two men sitting together and having a conversation. And the rest is history. They eventually married and had three daughters.

At the time, my father was responsible for taking care of the guns for the Nationalist Party. He had five cadets underneath him that he had to train. As he was highly skilled, he used to teach them how to shoot, how to throw a knife, how to do a bullseye, and how to throw the machete to a bullseye. He also taught them how to clean the guns well and oil them up. And then, he would take them to the beach and hide them in the sand.

One day, my mother was home alone, doing her chores for the day. A neighbor came running towards her house and informed her about the FBI and how they were going door to door, conducting a home search for people who were in possession of weapons.

Scared for her life, my frail mother, who was barely five feet tall, grabbed all the heavy firearms and threw them in the outhouse that was outside our house. When my father came back home, she told him everything that had happened that day. She was really shaken up by it, and seeing the state she was in, my father immediately comforted her. He took action right after and got the guns out. He cleaned them all up, boiled them, and put them back where they were supposed to be - back in the sand.

My parents' personality meshed in really well. It was like putting all the puzzle pieces perfectly in place. They had a strong bond that was sealed tightly with devotion to one another. Quite simply, my father was crazy about her. My mother was a shy, quiet woman who put a little seriousness into everything, while my father was the opposite of that. Though he was an introvert, his witty personality won the hearts of everyone who knew him. He enjoyed every moment and would take out all the seriousness that my mother would try to impose. He was funny and would always make jokes, never failing to make my mother smile. That is the kind of love they had for each other.

Then came the massacre of 1950, the year in which I was born. People from the Nationalist Party had asked my dad not to participate in any political activities during that time because he would have had to leave his two baby daughters behind. My mother had a bad feeling about it and didn't want him to go. But when the president told him to stay home, he couldn't argue with him. It was going to be bloody indeed.

Within the party, there was a member who owned a barbershop. At times, he would hold meetings in the back of his shop. One night, as he was closing it up, he walked towards the front of the shop. When he looked outside, he was startled to see that the police and FBI had surrounded his shop. Soon after, they started shooting in his direction with heavy machine guns. All of that for one person. The police riddled the shop with as much ammo as they possibly could. But they got shot back! They were met with firing, and it came from the barber. They found it unbelievable that by shooting a single person with as much ammo as they carried, there should have been nobody alive to shoot back at them. It was difficult to process that. They left after a few hours, scratching their heads in disbelief.

The barber was hiding above the door where you would install a fan to cool the place during the hot, humid months. Up in his hideout, he was at an advantage because he had a good view of the location. With his exceptional aim, he managed to fire at the FBI and the police. He had sustained two bullet wounds on his arm that day, but that was the extent of his injuries. He survived and became a hero of the party.

There had been massacres in Puerto Rico before this, too—one in 1926 and another in 1930. The most recent massacre, which happened in 1950, was the main reason my parents moved to Chicago to start anew. Since my dad had built and sold the dollhouses for a good amount of money, we barely ever had any financial problems. My parents started working right after, and we didn't have to ask for a single penny. They didn't go to welfare and paid for everything they had. We weren't rich, but we weren't poor either; we had a good life. I remember growing up in Chicago and loving every ounce of oxygen I breathed.

Although we were financially stable there, hard times hit us back in Puerto Rico. In the early years of my life, my parents worked extremely hard to make life comfortable for us. I remember when I was around two or three years of age, my father used to work as a construction worker. Oftentimes, he would come home really late. One time, he came home when the night was bleak. We didn't have dinner that night, and my father had returned with a single loaf of bread. My mother heated it, and we dunked it in our hot chocolate. My father had a difficult time finding work that paid well. Moreover, our family welcomed a new member to the house at the time, and now my mother had to stay at home and look after three babies.

We moved a lot when we first came to Chicago, up until we arrived in a very good neighborhood. We finally settled there, and we went to a private Catholic school. My mother wanted us to receive a good education; she was very serious about it, which is why she worked so hard.

English, however, stood as an imposing obstacle in my parents' daily lives. They used to go to a night school when they were younger to get a hold of the language, but something came up, and they were unable to attend any longer. They could understand some of it, but not enough to hold conversations or communicate well. While my father was building kitchen cabinets for work, he made a friend there. He was the one who taught him how to order ham and cheese, which my father ultimately got sick of.

Owing to his wits, my father had a magnetic presence. People naturally gravitated towards him. Since he was around so many people all the time, he was eventually able to learn the language little by little. While attending night school in the United States, my mother had picked up English, and because of that, she spoke it way better than my father. On the other hand, my father learned how to be a mechanic. So, on top of the fact that he was a carpenter, he now had mechanics under his belt, too.

# Chapter 5:

# Political Activism

The Puerto Rican Nationalist Party insurgency was a series of well-planned uprisings against U.S. government control over the island nation, spearheaded by Don Pedro Albizu Campos, the party's president, and intended to force Puerto Rico's separation. The "Free Associated State" (Estado Libre Asociado) status, which was implemented in 1950 and viewed by Nationalists as an extension of colonialism, was rejected by the party.

On October 30, 1950, the party planned a number of uprisings that were to occur in different Puerto Rican cities. Strong land and air forces, including U.S. military forces led by Major General Luis R. Esteves of the Puerto Rico National Guard, put an end to the uprisings. In a related incident, two New York City Nationalists tried in vain to storm the Blair House on November 1st of that year in an attempt to assassinate U.S. President Harry S. Truman. Truman backed the Puerto Rican government's efforts to draft a constitution that would rename the local government as a commonwealth of the United States and grant some degree of local autonomy.

My father's connection with the Nationalist Party traces back to the stories he had heard as a child, narrated by his father's close friend, Dr. Arvizu Campos. As he reached the age of 17, he found himself deeply entrenched in the Nationalist Party. This, however, stirred quite a commotion, having raised concerns for both his mother and mine. His mother, not very thrilled about the idea, tried to persuade him not to take part, but his determination prevailed. His passion was fueled by the vision of Puerto Rico standing independently, much like other Caribbean islands, each with its own government.

The historical backdrop added complexity to the struggle. Puerto Rico had undertaken a journey from Spanish rule to becoming part of the U.S. after the Spanish-American War, marked by shifting allegiances and attempts to establish local governance. The aftermath left Puerto Ricans grappling with a new reality, abruptly tethered to the United States.

As part of the party, my father assumed charge of 25 cadets. Under his mentorship, the cadets underwent a unique education, learning not just discipline but also the delicate balance between respectability and a particular covert mastery. Their backgrounds varied; some were from good homes instilled with respect, and others were highly educated. The party demanded a certain class from those who represented it and had some strict rules.

You were expected to keep a low profile, avoid making noise, and steer clear of loud or rude behavior. Laughter and joking weren't encouraged; the party preferred a quiet, reserved demeanor, emphasizing class. Hence, it was crucial to represent the party in this dignified manner. If you were too outgoing or drew too much attention, they didn't hesitate to show you the door. My father, having grown up with these principles, was well aware of the expectations. He knew how to carry himself, having understood the importance of adhering to these guidelines from an early age.

Through political upheaval and personal sacrifice, my father emerged as a resilient figure, facing a turbulent chapter in Puerto Rican history with courage and strategic wisdom.

Things escalated in 1950 when the party rallied for Puerto Rican independence, advocating for the recognition of an 1898 charter on Economy and Puerto Rico International Sovereignty. The revolts began on October 30th, 1950, following orders from the President and D.C. Grandfathers. While attempting to enter the White House through a side door, the party members were met with CIA firepower. All three—two men and a lady, were fatally shot on the spot.

It was right in the midst of these events that I made my entrance into the world in January 1950. Three years later, our journey led us to Chicago, a backdrop of political upheaval framing the milestones of my family's narrative.

My parents began saving up, and before long, they proudly owned a big building with four apartments. I remember how I'd go downstairs to my dad's shop, where he handcrafted kitchen cabinets. On the other hand, my mom, a skilled seamstress, always had a dream – her own bridal shop. Fifteen, maybe twenty years later, that dream indeed came true. She had her own bridal shop, just like she'd always wished for. However, the passage of time in between, particularly those years of my father's involvement in the party, was eventful, to say the least.

Caught the middle of this ensuing chaos, my mother, standing alongside my grandmother, shared in the concern for my father's safety. His attendance at party meetings, often culminating in late-night returns, invoked a constant worry. The fear stemmed not just from political tensions but the tangible threat of being followed, a chilling scenario where running out of nervousness could result in a gunshot to the back.

As my father was a grown man, his mom couldn't boss him around anymore. Once he married my mom, it made him realize that he had a wife and three little girls to look out for, and he couldn't risk leaving my mom a widow. So, he trod carefully, becoming more mindful of his actions.

After the heartbreaking incident with the three Puerto Ricans at the White House, the party planned another protest, expecting it to turn chaotic. The president of the party, aware of my father's family, insisted he stay home, considering the well-being of his three little girls and wife. Despite his desire to be there, he wisely chose not to argue with the party president and stayed home. My mom felt a huge sense of relief knowing he wasn't going to be in the midst of potential danger. The moment when she found out he didn't have to go brought her even more relief.

Yet, my father's bravery and intellect became guiding lights in these challenging times. He navigated the thin line between passion and prudence, understanding that drawing attention to oneself could be dangerous. There were no late-night bar escapes for him because it would have been a deliberate choice against the party's principles.

After the war, our journey led us to a new home in Chicago. We, the three Americanized girls, had become so immersed in the U.S. lifestyle that he realized Puerto Rico might not be the best fit for us. It was despite the island's advancements that made it almost like America, with highways, skyscrapers, and everything reminiscent of Chicago.

We didn't return to Puerto Rico until my father was in his 70s, choosing it as his final resting place, where he eventually passed away at the ripe age of 76 due to complications from diabetes. A car accident marked the unfortunate turn of events, triggered by a sudden and severe drop in his blood sugar levels. Dizziness overcame him, leading to the collision of his car with eight others before ultimately crashing into a pole. The internal injuries sustained from the accident proved fatal, leading to his demise.

During my childhood, my father was a lively and expressive man. When he would get upset, he'd raise his voice and yell, creating an atmosphere that frightened me. Loud confrontations were my Achilles' heel, and I found solace in my mother's quiet and reserved demeanor, reflecting her calmness.

Unlike my two sisters, I was deeply affected by the loudness, making it challenging for me to have a close relationship with my father. I kept my distance, fearful of his outbursts. As I grew older, I came to understand that my father's strictness during my upbringing was his way of imparting discipline. It wasn't until I married and had children of my own that I gained a clearer perspective on his intentions and the values he instilled in us girls.

I began to see him from the lens of a parent. We bonded closely, a connection that strengthened in my late 20s, and from then on, we became exceptionally close. I cherish this closeness because when he passed away, I felt gratitude for the quality time we had shared.

During those later years, he opened up to me about aspects of his life, particularly the intricate details of his involvement with the party. It was a revelation, a topic he had never broached with us before. I decided to look my father up on the internet, using his first, middle, and last names, as well as his mother's last name, as per the customary naming norms in Puerto Rico. However, I discovered a narrative that transcended all expectations.

The initial shock hit me like a wave when the search results revealed a startling statement – "wanted by the FBI." My heart just dropped, and with a sense of dread, I delved into the horrors that the information the internet provided me with.

The online records provided a detailed account, including extensive files related to my father and others associated with the political party. I was surprised that the FBI had paid more attention to my father than even the party president. This increased scrutiny was mainly due to his lifelong affiliation with the party, which had its roots in his upbringing since childhood.

One notable incident that emerged from these files recounted an attempted arrest on non-compliance with army enlistment charges. My father, however, swiftly challenged this accusation, urging the authorities to scrutinize their records more thoroughly.

Upon a careful review, they acknowledged an error and promptly released him.

It was quite interesting to find out that the U.S. Army repeatedly rejected my father's enlistment during World War II. According to the records, this was due to his poor eyesight. However, this irony struck me because, in reality, he was an excellent sharpshooter and was known for his exceptional precision. He even boasted about his ability to throw knives with pinpoint accuracy. The contradiction between the official narrative of his eyesight issues and his demonstrated abilities raises intriguing questions.

After discovering something new, I experienced a surreal moment. It made me realize how different official records can be from the reality of my father's exceptional skills. This experience showed me how complicated misunderstandings can become when someone's history is tied up with politics and unique abilities.

When I learned of the FBI's interest in him, I was left with disbelief. At that time, he was in Puerto Rico while I was still residing in the States. Regrettably, I never had the chance to discuss the things I discovered about him with him. The physical distance acted as a barrier, and this should remind others not to put off talking to parents about their past. When the realization finally sets in, long after they're gone, many unanswerable questions arise.

After reflecting on my own experience, I encourage others to talk with their parents before it's too late. Parents have many untold stories and insights that often go unexplored, so it's important not to miss out on these opportunities.

# Chapter 6:

# Relocating to the United States

My father's luck did not ignite in Puerto Rico. He would always be looking for work, but the chances of getting a job there were slim then. His brother, Morgan Ledger, wrote him a letter asking him to move to Chicago since many career opportunities awaited him.

The situation had gotten so bad that he would often return home empty-handed. My father had no choice but to listen to my uncle's advice. We sold the dollhouses, and the money we got from it helped us start a new life in a different country, surrounded by unfamiliar faces. It was quite overwhelming, but my parents were resilient; they did everything to provide a better life for us girls.

Just a day after we landed in Chicago, both my parents were employed. However, there was a language barrier since English is predominantly spoken in the States. Gradually, they started learning, went to school, and gained a good command of the language. My mother, especially, had gotten quite proficient, although her English still hinted at her nationality owing to her accent. I was a baby when she was attending classes, so it was impressive that she cared for me and was dedicated to learning simultaneously.

On the other hand, my father went to McCann Technical School in Chicago and opened an automobile repair shop, hoping it would bring in fortune. Let's just say that it didn't go very well. Still, after selling his business, he bought the whole building, so I wouldn't consider it a grave loss.

Moving to Chicago was a good decision because it was more than our little family that depended on him. My grandmother and my father's sisters also needed financial aid. Hence, my father became responsible for them on top of my mother and us three girls.

When the business failed, my father returned to looking for employment catering to his carpentry skills. So, his work and night school kept him occupied. He worked when the sun was out, and he would disappear with the sun by night. The fruit of his hard work was right around the corner, and I could feel it.

My mother's mother also lived in Chicago, so we lived with her initially. Some of my relatives, whom I was unfamiliar with, lived in my grandmother's place, too. My cousins, Victor, Blanche, and their parents then moved into a two-room apartment, and my father wanted to secure a space of his own as well.

Once the renovation and changes were complete, they swiftly moved. Soon after that, we got our own apartment. Every year, we would move to a place better than the last one.

I was only three at the time we shifted to Chicago. I was the youngest among three children, the oldest being six. She had to start school right away because she was older than the regular kids when they started school. Our sudden shift left us concerned because none of us knew English in the slightest. Therefore, it was a given that going to school would be troubling.

My mother insisted on the idea of us going to a Catholic school since she prioritized education over everything else. Money didn't matter when it came to education; so much was out of their pockets every year. I appreciate my parents' hard work and consideration for us in every aspect. They never let us feel poor regardless of our financial situation. We always felt loved and surrounded by warmth.

A vast portion of school life involves social interaction with peers – forming friendships, bonding over lessons, and finding camaraderie through extracurricular activities. However, it becomes difficult for children to mix in when they cannot speak the language.

It makes you feel left out and unable to enjoy school. Since we started school right after settling in, it took us a while to fit in the crowd and not feel like an alien. It is a good thing that children are easily able to fill up that language barrier gap in a short period, unlike adults who struggle to adapt well or quickly.

When my parents started receiving their income, they began spending it on decorating our home. We could afford our own place and made it as homely as possible. Since then, our place constantly upgraded to a better one, and we had completely forgotten about when we couldn't even afford to eat dinner and make ends meet with stale bread.

Now, we were putting up wallpapers, wall decors, and other things that seemed like a distant world in the past. We then decided to put up cabinets in the kitchen, and my dad's ears stood straight when he heard of this decision. He was on a mission now: to make cabinets that would break the ice every time someone visited us. He was successful, and even the people who owned that apartment loved those cabinets.

Although my parents would pool all the money to get a better place every year, we still had some money to enjoy the present one. I remember our visit to the park every weekend.

Lincoln Park ran alongside Lake Michigan on the North Side of Chicago, Illinois. Its name was changed from Cemetery Park to Lincoln after the assassination of President Abraham Lincoln. There were two museums and a zoo in the oldest part of the park. This place was so big that it had nature reserves, harbors, beaches, and recreational facilities, including pitches and courts for many sports.

There was so much to do there that I could not have enough of it. Every weekend was a new, fresh experience. Not a single day was boring, and we always looked forward to going out and spending quality time together.

My parents never let their guard down near us, even though it was so difficult to immigrate and settle in a country with unknown people and a language we had never spoken before.

It was like entering a confusing world when my parents first came to this new place. It was tough to fit in with everyone and pay attention to everything around them. Every move they made was hard because they were learning the unwritten rules of a completely new society. They were always looking for signs.

Making friends in a new culture is not easy either, especially when you're a well-established adult. You are always trying to connect with people, but it is often difficult because of the different backgrounds. This struggle to build good relationships in the midst of cultural differences would make anyone inclined to loneliness and isolation.

On top of that, dealing with the language was another challenge, as I mentioned before. People like shopkeepers, government workers, employers, and teachers aren't patient when talking to immigrants. It makes it even harder to make real connections. Every day feels like a battle to fit in and be understood.

Dealing with all these challenges made my parents see that it wasn't just about them adjusting to a new culture. It was really about everyone, both new and old community members, working together to understand each other and make genuine connections.

As my parents continued their journey, they understood that finding people who care about you amid all the overwhelming feelings needs your strength. It is not just about fitting in but about recognizing that we all share our humanity, regardless of language or culture.

I applaud my parents for being fighters and successfully tackling life's challenges before and after moving to Chicago. To me, they are heroes who quietly withstood the struggles and managed to give us a life that was not only peaceful but also loving.

# Chapter 7:

# Entrepreneurial Ventures

When my father first settled on starting his own business, it was an ambitious undertaking, but not without significant challenges. As someone who had worked as an employee for many years, going down his own path meant venturing into the unfamiliar arena of entrepreneurship.

The financial risks loomed large, but my father was ready to jump these hurdles, driven by a desire to secure himself and his family. Perhaps our struggles in Puerto Rico were difficult for him to bear, and he didn't want us to live on stale bread again. It truly warmed my heart towards him, realizing that despite his affection for us, it was his hard work that solidified the love he had for his family.

Although my father was successful in building the foundations of his business, marketing the fledgling company seemed daunting without a sizable advertising budget at his disposal. However, perhaps his biggest concern was shouldering all the responsibilities of being a sole proprietor. He knew he would handle every aspect of operations daily, from sales and customer service to bookkeeping and ordering inventory. Looking back, considering all the roles he needed to fill, it must have been hard not to feel overwhelmed.

While he poured his heart and soul into the journey of bringing his vision to life, the early years proved an uphill battle. The business struggled to become profitable, and because of that, day-to-day pressures and long-term sustainability concerns grew.

As much as my father wanted to see the company succeed, he realized running it was taking a toll on him both financially and mentally. After much soul-searching, he made the tough decision to sell the business, not wanting to risk further losses. It must have been quite disappointing to end this chapter, but my father never once returned home looking stressed or frustrated; he always had his happy face on whenever he was around us. After all, he was resilient, always looking at the bright side. His willingness to learn prevailed over failure, and he moved on without regret or being intimidated by the setback.

Over time, my father was determined to try business ownership again. With the funds gained from selling his first company, he and my mother were able to see an opportunity. A multi-unit building was for sale, and my father knew buying it would benefit us. So, my mother borrowed some money from her job's union and took a risk with my father. They invested their savings, becoming landlords of four apartments, helping provide a steady income stream.

However, my father's skills lay in carpentry, which had been honed from years of experience, and he wanted to make use of what he had perfected. He decided to launch a carpentry business and a remodeling and repair job. He started small - from the basement of the new building - and steadily grew his clientele through hard work and quality craftsmanship. Now, he was no longer saddled with the pressures of a startup, and this new business began witnessing its envisioned success.

Even though the carpentry business was now thriving, my father began feeling drawn back to his homeland of Puerto Rico. Perhaps it was the familiar culture and beauty of the land that he missed so deeply or that it held his childhood and many fond memories.

He genuinely contemplated moving the whole family back, wanting to return to what felt like home. But when he looked at his three young daughters, who were Americanized by this time in how they spoke, acted, and viewed the world, he realized it simply wouldn't work. And he was right; we had become too accustomed to life in the States to uproot ourselves at this juncture.

The transition would be extremely difficult because we had moved to America at such a young age, and settling in Puerto Rico would mean leaving our way of life to settle into a completely different one. I recall when he shared his thoughts of moving, we thought it was the craziest idea and disapproved of it, but later, I realized that he must really have been missing the place he was brought up in.

On top of that, he was a family man through and through. If an outside family member struggled to put food on their table, especially if there were children, my father would intervene and ensure they were fed for the time being. He would even leave them with some money if they needed something other than food.

Thinking about how much he cared for those around him, it must have pained him to give up his dream of returning. However, my father's selfless, caring nature shone through in his decision to prioritize our stability, happiness, and future opportunities over his own nostalgia. He resolved to cherish the place he came from while building our lives where we were. As much as a piece of his heart remained in Puerto Rico, his family had to come first.

My father loved his country, but he also learned to love the USA by learning how to raise his three daughters in the big city of Chicago. I love that city. I have fond memories of playing on the streets of Chicago with my sister, Mickie. It might have been his trait that I carried to be a patriot. Just like him, I wish to own a house in Ponce, Puerto Rico, and continue the legacy that he has left behind.

Reflecting on it with the wisdom of experience and age, I realize just how correct my father's instincts were. While we visited Puerto Rico occasionally as children and enjoyed the warm culture and beaches, we truly had become outsiders there in many ways. The pace of life, daily customs, and even simple things like the Spanish-only environment would have been extraordinarily difficult for us, who were accustomed to American society. I know that culturally, we would have felt like foreigners in my father's homeland.

Moreover, the school system, activities, foods, and general lifestyle were so different from what we knew. We likely would have resented leaving everything familiar behind and be miserable about that drastic change of scenery. Cultural shock, especially as teenagers, would have caused irreparable damage to our relationships and development.

So, after decades of hard work building his carpentry business and providing for our family through rental properties, my father's diligence paid off. As the real estate market boomed, he decided to sell the building, earning a sizable profit from the investment he and my mother had made all those years ago.

Finally, with his business doing well and savings secure, my father was able to enjoy retirement. He took great joy in watching his daughters grow into adulthood, forge their careers, and start their own families. He was growing old happily, but as life did what it did, his body grew weaker, too. Even then, my father's mind and spirit remained alive, and he took pride and satisfaction in being surrounded by grandchildren for whom he made sacrifices so that he could give them the best life.

Still, none of us could have predicted the sudden turn of events one fateful morning. My father woke up with chest pains and later collapsed. After we rushed him to the hospital, we were told by the doctors that it was a massive heart attack and his arteries were severely clogged. It was devastating to see him, who once was such an energetic person, lying on a hospital bed, fighting for his life. I didn't want him to leave us in such a painful way and begged the doctors to ease his struggles. He told us that my father would need surgery immediately to become stable, and without hesitation, we agreed to it.

Every second in the operating room was torturous to us. My father was fighting a battle of life and death, and all we could do was pray for him to come out well. After hours of waiting, the doctor came out of the room, and we immediately went up to him to ask about my father's condition. It was a relief to see the doctor's calm expression, who told us that the quadruple bypass surgery had been successful in saving my father's life.

While we hoped for a full recovery, it became clear to us that the ordeal had forever changed him. Though grateful for more time, he got tired easily and lacked his previous vigor. It pained us all to see him so diminished in stark contrast with the towering figure of our childhoods. But his gentle smile and loving nature remained unchanged.

In his final years, our focus turned to providing comfort, making memories, and expressing our deep gratitude for the gift of his life. We decided it was best that my parents moved back to where they had come from, Puerto Rico, so they could live the rest of their lives peacefully in a place so close to their hearts.

Eventually, the end drew near, and my father passed away at the age of 76, having lived a full life.

As I mentioned earlier, my father had been quite active in Puerto Rico's nationalist party during his youth, and through his commitment to advocating for Puerto Rican issues, he gained much respect from his fellow members and leaders. Decades later, when my father returned to Puerto Rico in his final years, that respect for him remained alive. Upon learning of his passing, the nationalist party wanted to honor the man who had contributed so much to their cause in his early days.

So, they arranged for a special radio announcement to be made, notifying the entire community of my father's death. The party's tribute could be heard across the streets of the land, on radios, and from the mouths of the people, celebrating his memory and legacy. Seeing how meaningful his involvement had been brought me comfort and pride. Even after so much time away, he was still remembered with high regard by the movement he once served. Without a shadow of a doubt, I can say that their public memorial was a most deserving and beautiful recognition.

# Chapter 8:

# Family Man and Community Leader

Upon reflection, not many could live the way my father did. With tireless dedication and relentless passion, he poured his whole self into trying to make life better for others. It was never merely a job to him - it was a calling, a sacred duty to assist anyone in need, no matter the personal cost. He worked endless hours and took on responsibilities that would have broken lesser men, but he found purpose and fulfillment in improving people's lives through compassionate service.

Most importantly, for all his devotion to his community's welfare, he never neglected what mattered most - his own loved ones at home. No matter how intense the demands of his work, he always made sure to be fully present and engaged with his family. They gave him the strength and renewal to return each day and take up his charge with renewed energy. Thus, his life was led selflessly but sustainably, with deep care for countrymen and family.

His passion and love towards us and others oozed out of him in a way that left no doubt regarding how deeply he felt about everything. He was not afraid to show affection towards his family, reflected in his tender words of care, support, and pride— yet the quieter, subtler things always spoke even louder. As I mentioned, he was often on the go, working tirelessly toward his duties, but he made certain to carve out small moments wherever possible. Whether it was an extra hug before rushing off, a kiss on the forehead as he tucked us in, fleeting hand squeezes, and lingering gazes, these silent demonstrations reinforced what his heart probably already articulated. We felt the strength of his love in its constancy, in how reliably he was there for every momentous occasion, challenge, or joy despite his busy schedule. Actions indeed always spoke volumes as far as he was concerned, but his presence alone assured us that we were the most important people in his world.

When he was young, he was deeply aware of the suffering in his community from the beginning. With his few resources, he worked to alleviate as much of it as possible. He looked out for neighbors and rallied people together; with that, he managed to create a support network during hardship. His small acts of compassion, such as ensuring people had extra money for other essentials, showed his profound empathy even at such a vulnerable, impressionable age.

When opportunity called us to a new homeland, he nimbly incorporated his drive for justice into union advocacy – but on his own terms, with family firmly anchored as his top priority. While it is uncommon for people in positions of responsibility to lose themselves to fleeting pleasures, my father shunned such distractions, seeing greater meaning in simple acts of service at home.

Instead of wasting evenings indulging in drinks and spending the nights with friends, as some dared mock, he was always by my mother's side, gladly handling domestic tasks alongside her.

I'll never forget walking into the house and finding him diligently scrubbing floors. Such acts lifted my mother's burdens and undermined superficial notions of what constituted "men's work." My father knew that behind every strong man lay an equally commendable partner, and he endlessly honored my mother's contributions through compassionate companionship and care.

The example they set by selflessly working together has always stayed with me and reminded me that what truly matters most realizes its purpose, not in flashy distraction but in filling loved ones' lives with comfort, stability, and joy. To this day, I vividly remember the cozy warmth of steam rising as my mother gently bathed us, her soft voice mingling with the sounds of my father's efficient, familiar movements as he readied our uniforms nearby. They were united in their dedication to our well-being. Consequently, even mundane chores took on a lighter air when done together, infused with mutual unspoken affection.

The contentment my parents found in one another's company and duties held joyfully as a team has left me with reflections as comforting now as they were then. Though responsibilities called, their hearts were in sync with their family, and in this lay the secret of our happiness. What greater gift could parents give children than bringing such stability, teamwork, and love to the home? Needless to say, I remain eternally grateful for the shining example they became for us. My father's love was not just limited to us; our children were also bestowed with his affection. My children would call my father "Tata." He was always very happy that, despite having only three daughters, each of us gave him a grandson. But he was particularly fond of my daughter, Nicole. He was crazy about her and would shower her with love.

Growing up, I was afraid of my father because he had a bad temper. Being the youngest, he didn't come at me like he did with my sisters, especially the oldest, who would often go head-to-head with him. I stayed away from him because he was boisterous and loud, while I was quiet and timid. As a result, we often moved in opposite directions, avoiding conflict.

We developed a beautiful relationship that lasted until the day he died. We became very close, and he started sharing stories about his life, including his involvement in the nationalist party, which he had never discussed with his daughters. I learned so many things from both of my parents and applied many of those lessons to raising my own children. There were numerous great things I remembered and cherished.

My father was always worried that we would get hurt. I remember the first time he caught me roller-skating. He yelled at me, worried because I was skating on the street. He said, "From what I can see, you know how to ride them really well," but he was mad because I borrowed a friend's skates. I was too nervous to eat during dinner that night, anticipating a possible spanking.

After dinner, he called me into his bedroom and told me to get dressed. I asked where we were going, and he said we were going to Sears to buy my own roller skates. Despite his initial anger, he wanted to support my passion. He bought me a pair of roller skates that evening.

We weren't allowed to ride bikes or swim, but I was the first to ride a bike and the first to swim. Even though he didn't want us to do those activities, he was always very proud of my achievements. I pursued them on my own, proving my determination and independence, and he recognized that.

Reflecting on these moments, I realize how my father's love and concern were always present, even when cloaked in strictness and worry. They say a father's love is the backbone of a family. He nurtures each child with boundless affection and wisdom; through his kindness, patience, and unwavering support, he leaves a deep mark on their hearts. His love is a source of strength, empowering each of them to embrace their uniqueness and confidently pursue their dreams. His guidance shapes their values, teaching them the importance of integrity, empathy, and resilience.

# Chapter 9:

# Tragedy and Legacy

The journey through love, loss, and resilience is much like the unfolding of a rainbow across the sky. Each stage of the journey brings forth a different hue, creating a spectrum of emotions and experiences that together form the richness of life.

In the beginning, love appears as vibrant as sunrise, full of warmth and promises. It is the first blush of dawn, the red and orange hues that signify the start of a new day. This is the time of connection, discovering a soulmate, and building dreams together. Just as the rainbow's colors blend seamlessly into one another, so do two lives intertwine, creating a beautiful harmony that feels destined and timeless.

However, as life progresses, the shades deepen and diversify, reflecting the shared experiences. Together, all the colors capture the essence of a life in companionship and partnership. But, like a rainbow that eventually fades, loss enters the scene with the blues and indigos, representing the sorrow and grief that accompany the departure of a loved one. Yet, just as every rainbow must give way to the light, this darkness too shall pass, though its imprint remains forever on the soul.

Resilience is the arc that connects the colors, the bridge between the joy of love and the pain of loss. It is the ability to find strength in the darkest moments, to remember the vivid colors of love even when they seem distant.

My own life has been a vivid reflection of this spectrum. When we faced the reality that we would never return to Puerto Rico as a family, it felt like stepping into a new world, one full of possibilities but also challenges. Leaving behind the familiar landscapes of our homeland, we ventured into uncharted territory, embracing the uncertainty and the promise of a fresh start.

While adjusting to new waves, a few years passed by, and my older sister, Esther, found love. Her engagement was a beacon of joy and hope, symbolizing the blending of cultures and the creation of new traditions. About five to six months later, she married an American man and began her journey in this new land.

Eight months after Esther's wedding, my sister Mickie followed suit and married. Her wedding added another layer of celebration and adaptation to our lives. Meanwhile, I watched and waited, taking in the excitement and the changes around me. I waited two years after Mickie's wedding to have my own, a time filled with anticipation and preparation.

Those three years were a whirlwind of matrimonial festivities, constant celebration, and adjustment. The time was nothing less than a reflection of all the bright colors of the rainbow. On the other hand, my poor parents were immersed in the frenzy of wedding preparations.

My mother became our family's wedding dressmaker with the skills she had acquired in Puerto Rico, where she met my father. She lovingly crafted Mickie's wedding dress; when it was my turn, she also made mine. I adored my dress, complete with a long Cathedral veil, reflecting my mother's talent and love.

My husband Nick and I met when we were juniors in high school. The following year, we graduated, and six months later, he was drafted into the Army. He tested high in Electronics and Mechanics. I begged him to pursue Electronics because everyone was studying computers then. Nick just wanted to serve in the Army for two years and get it over with, but the Vietnam War was intense. Fearing for his safety, I begged him to join the Air Force instead, where the likelihood of being sent to Vietnam was lower. He signed up for four years in the Air Force to alleviate my fears.

Our journey together took us to various places. Nick attended school in the Air Force for a year, and after that, we were assigned to a new location each year. We started in Denver, Colorado, which we both loved.

After Denver, we were stationed in Indiana, which we both hated. Next came the Philippines, where we were living in luxury. We were there for eighteen months, and during this time, I was pregnant with our first baby. Although we were far from home, our lifestyle there made us feel like we were rich people.

Following our time in the Philippines, we were stationed in Georgia, where our daughter was born. This marked the end of our four years in the Air Force. We returned home, and Nick landed his dream job in the elevator industry, thus providing a great living for our family. Two years later, I gave birth to our son.

Two years after his birth, we bought our first house in the suburbs after spending our entire lives in the big city of Chicago.

Nick and I were married for 50 years, in addition to the three years we spent together before getting married. Unfortunately, Nick had an accident at work, resulting in a neck injury when he was only 39 years old, which left him unable to work. This led him into a deep depression as he felt hopeless and useless. He underwent seven surgeries on his back and was constantly in pain.

One morning, as I was beginning my day and attending to household tasks, I went upstairs to ask Nick what he wanted for breakfast. To my shock, I found him holding a gun. My heart skipped a beat as I questioned him about it. He assured me he was only cleaning it, but his eyes betrayed a deeper chaos. With a heavy heart, he confessed that he felt like a piece of nothing. His words cut through me, revealing the depth of his pain and despair.

I looked into his eyes and told him with all sincerity that he was the best husband a woman could ever hope for. I hoped my words would reach him, comforting him in his darkest moments. With a heavy heart, I went downstairs to make him breakfast, praying that my love and reassurance would be enough to help him find his way back to the light.

But the prayers seemed to go unanswered, and soon, the dreadful event I had feared most happened. For a moment, I wanted the clock to pause, to freeze time so I could find a way to prevent the inevitable.

That was when I heard the shot of the gun. I ran up the stairs, and there he was—Nick had taken his own life. In that instant, my world shattered. From that point on, my life has been marked by an overwhelming sense of loneliness, missing him so much every single day.

I live with my children, alternating between my son and daughter. Spending time with my grandchildren brings me joy, even though they are not little anymore. Their presence is a balm to my wounded heart. It's been four years since I became a widow, and though life goes on, the ache of his absence remains.